TECHNOLOGY DURING THE VIETNAM WAR

HEATHER C. HUDAK

Checkerboard
Library

An Imprint of Abdo Publishing
abdopublishing.com

ABDOPUBLISHING.COM

Published by Abdo Publishing, a division of ABDO, PO Box 398166, Minneapolis, Minnesota 55439. Copyright © 2017 by Abdo Consulting Group, Inc. International copyrights reserved in all countries. No part of this book may be reproduced in any form without written permission from the publisher. Checkerboard Library™ is a trademark and logo of Abdo Publishing.

Printed in the United States of America, North Mankato, Minnesota
102016
012017

THIS BOOK CONTAINS
RECYCLED MATERIALS

Content Developer: Nancy Tuminelly
Design and Production: Mighty Media, Inc.
Series Editor: Rebecca Felix
Cover Photo: AP Images
Interior Photos: AP Images, pp. 5, 9 (top), 15, 26; Getty Images, pp. 9 (bottom), 12, 23; Jorge Láscar/Flickr, p. 20; Shutterstock Images, pp. 5 (inset), 16–17; Wikimedia Commons, pp. 6, 8, 11, 19, 25, 29

Publisher's Cataloging-in-Publication Data

Names: Hudak, Heather C., author.
Title: Technology during the Vietnam War / by Heather C. Hudak.
Description: Minneapolis, MN : Abdo Publishing, 2017. | Series: Military technologies | Includes bibliographical references and index.
Identifiers: LCCN 2016944859 | ISBN 9781680784145 (lib. bdg.) | ISBN 9781680797671 (ebook)
Subjects: LCSH: United States--History--Vietnam War, 1961-1975--Technology--Juvenile literature. | Technology--United States--History--20th century--Juvenile literature.
Classification: DDC 959.704--dc23
LC record available at http://lccn.loc.gov/2016944859

CONTENTS

NORTH VS. SOUTH

The Vietnamese people battled for many years, first for independence, and then in civil war. France had controlled Vietnam from the late 1800s. In 1940, Japan conquered the area, but allowed French authorities to continue to govern.

Japan took direct control in 1945, only to have France take it back in 1946. But the Vietnamese were tired of being ruled by other nations. They wanted freedom.

Around this time, a new leader rose to power in Vietnam. Ho Chi Minh had studied communism. He wanted to rule Vietnam using this form of government.

Ho formed the League for the Independence of Vietnam, or Viet Minh, in 1941. He proclaimed Vietnam's independence. The French opposed. In 1946, the First Indochina War began between the Viet Minh and France.

The Viet Minh won the war in 1954. Peace **negotiations** split Vietnam in two. Ho controlled

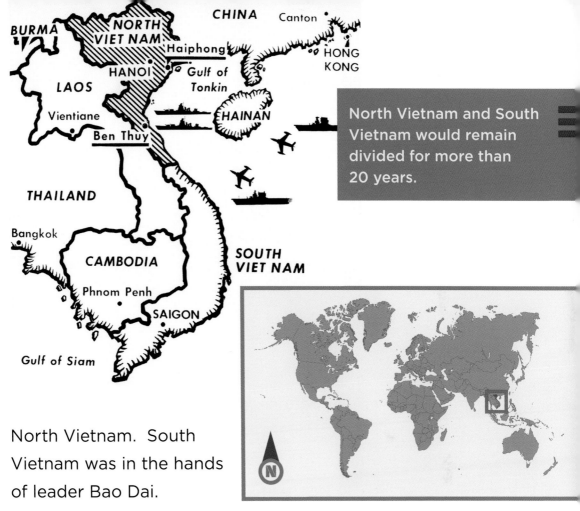

North Vietnam and South Vietnam would remain divided for more than 20 years.

North Vietnam. South Vietnam was in the hands of leader Bao Dai.

In 1956, Ngo Dinh Diem came to power in the South. Diem opposed communism. And he feared it would spread from the North.

The United States also opposed communism. Beginning in the 1950s, it sent US military advisors to South Vietnam. The advisors shared **tactics** for battling the Viet Minh.

US and South Vietnamese troops advance on an NLF camp in 1965. The NLF drew its enemy to isolated, rural areas.

In the meantime, some South Vietnamese began supporting the Viet Minh. These supporters were called the National Liberation Front (NLF). Diem called them the Vietcong.

In August 1964, two US ships reported being attacked by North Vietnam. In March 1965, the United States sent soldiers to Vietnam. It had officially joined the Vietnam War. The war was fought between two sides, each made up of several armies. US troops battled alongside the South Vietnamese army. The NLF, Viet Minh, and North Vietnamese Army (NVA) fought against them.

The US military had to adapt to a new type of **warfare** during the war. The NLF used **guerilla** warfare. US troops were more familiar with **conventional** warfare.

US soldiers also had to adapt to Vietnam's **terrain** and hot climate. The terrain varied from muddy jungles to rugged mountains. Soldiers needed special weapons and **vehicles** that held up in these conditions.

Guns and tanks were made sturdier to persist in the harsh conditions. New forms of chemical weapons helped troops cut through jungle trees. In the air, **fleets** of jet fighters gave US and South Vietnamese troops the edge.

Helicopters also played an important role in the war. Soldiers relied on them for transportation as well as offensive support during ground battles. These **technologies** were key in gaining advantage and saving lives during more than ten years of battle.

1941

Communist leader Ho Chi Minh founds the Viet Minh.

1954

Vietnam is split in two at the end of the First Indochina War.

1950s

The US military sends advisors to South Vietnam.

AUGUST 1964

Two US ships report that they are attacked by North Vietnam. US Congress prepares to send troops to Vietnam.

1973

A **cease-fire** begins with the signing of the Paris Peace Accords. All remaining US troops leave Vietnam.

MARCH 1965

US combat troops arrive in Vietnam.

1968

The Tet Offensive occurs in January and February. More than 100 South Vietnamese towns are attacked.

1975

Saigon, the capital of South Vietnam, falls to the North.

INFANTRY VEHICLES

Ground battles during the Vietnam War were often small **skirmishes**. At first, most of this fighting took place in southern Vietnam. As the war continued, fighting moved north.

US and South Vietnamese **infantry** often used tanks to travel into ground combat. These massive war **vehicles** could travel over all types of **terrain**. They were covered in tough armor. Soldiers rode inside or on top of tanks, firing at the enemy using the tanks' rotating guns.

One US tank used during the war was the M48 Patton. It could move at a speed of 30 miles per hour (48 kmh). The tank's main gun could rotate to fire in any direction. Heavy armor protected the M48 from enemy fire.

The M113 armored **personnel** carrier was also important in ground

TECH FACT

More than 600 M48 Pattons were sent to Vietnam during the war.

combat. It was the military **vehicle** used most often by US and South Vietnamese troops.

The US-developed M113 was used to transport troops or supplies safely to a battlefield and

The M113 was often referred to as a "battle taxi" by troops.

then withdraw. Many military **vehicles** of the day were made of steel. But the M113 was made from **aluminum** alloy.

Alloy did not protect as well as steel against enemy fire. But it was much lighter weight. As a result, the M113 could be moved more easily from place to place.

The M113 was also an amphibious vehicle, meaning it could run on both land and water. This made the M113 great for **reconnaissance** missions. It could attack the

BATTLE OF THE PLAIN OF REEDS

In September 1962, the South Vietnamese army battled the NLF in the Plain of Reeds. This is a wetland in Vietnam's Mekong Delta. The army planned to use M113 armored personnel carriers in the attack. US military advisor Captain James W. Bricker reviewed their plan. He suggested the M113s not be used. Bricker was concerned the vehicles could not handle the soft, wet terrain. But the South Vietnamese army did not take his advice.

On September 25, South Vietnamese soldiers drove nine M113s across a canal. They attacked a group of NLF hiding in rice paddies. Bricker had also told the troops they should dismount the M113s during battle. But the South Vietnamese troops stayed atop the vehicles, charging right at the enemy.

The M113s splashed through the wet fields, scaring the NLF from hiding. Many NLF soldiers were terrified of the amphibious vehicles and fled. The South Vietnamese army eventually won the battle. This success led to the M113's widespread use by the South Vietnamese army for combat, rather than just transportation. Later, US troops fighting in Vietnam would adopt this tactic as well.

enemy in almost any place. Soldiers used the M113 to push through the thick jungle vegetation and across flooded rice paddies.

⫶(3)⫶
MACHINE GUNS

As they fought with or without war **vehicles**, **infantry fired at the enemy using powerful rifles.** The M16 rifle was an **automatic** weapon used by US ground troops. It held 20 to 30 bullets at a time, depending on the model.

Soldiers could reload the M16 easily while in combat. They could also set the rifle to automatic. On this setting, the M16 fired an estimated 600 to 700 bullets per minute.

US and South Vietnamese troops also used M60 machine guns. These guns held 100 pre-linked bullets that hung from the gun in a strip. Although it held more bullets than the M16, the M60 fired only 550 bullets per minute.

The M60 was also heavier than the M16. This made it more difficult to carry through Vietnam's thick forests and rivers. But unlike the M16, the M60 could be mounted onto stands and military vehicles. This allowed soldiers to fire with better control and **accuracy**.

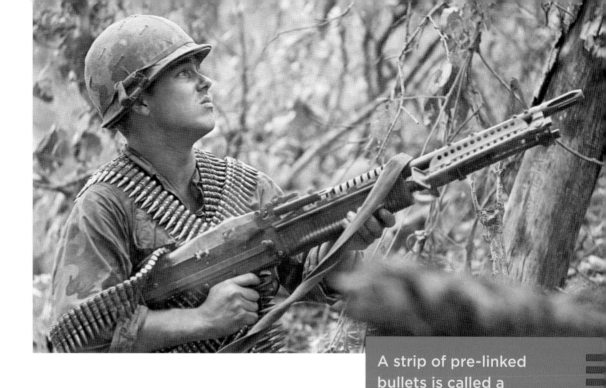

The M16 and M60 were far from
perfect, however. Neither model
held up well in Vietnam's wet,
muddy jungles. Soldiers could not
always obtain proper cleaning supplies. If these guns
weren't cleaned often, they jammed.

The NLF carried AK-47 assault rifles. They were easier
to use and maintain than M16s and M60s. But their range
and **accuracy** were not as good.

M60 MACHINE GUN

The M60 was most often fired from a mounted stand. But it could also be fired from the hip. Because the gun was quite heavy, it required two soldiers to operate. The one who would fire it was called the gunner. The second soldier was the assistant gunner. He carried the **ammunition** and helped load the gun.

LOADING

1. The gunner pulled the cover down. This was to make sure the cocking handle was forward.

2. The assistant gunner placed the first round of the bandolier in position.

3. The gunner pulled the cocking handle to the rear. This completed loading the ammunition.

FIRING

4. The gunner pulled the cocking handle forward. Using front and rear sights, he aimed at the target.

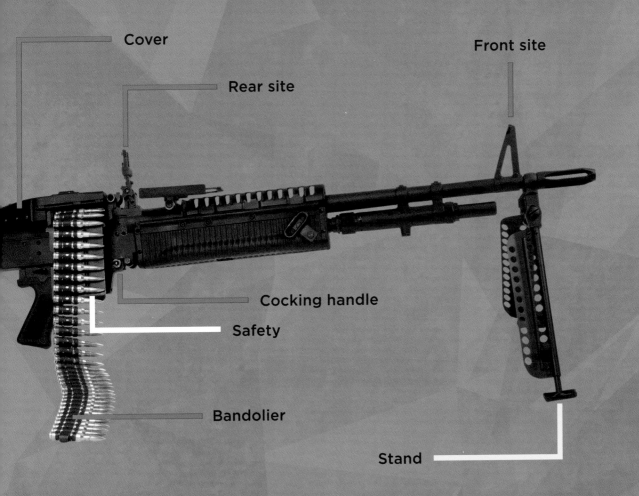

Cover

Rear site

Front site

Cocking handle

Safety

Bandolier

Stand

5. Next, the gunner unlocked the safety and pulled a small lever called the trigger. The gun would continue to fire while his finger was pressing the trigger, or until **ammunition** ran out.

6. The assistant gunner fed a new bandolier into the gun when ammunition ran out.

EXPLOSIVES AND TRAPS

Guns weren't the only **ammunition** soldiers carried in combat. They also had grenades. These handheld explosives were activated by pulling out a pin at the top. Then a soldier would throw the grenade toward the enemy. After a few seconds, it would explode.

Mark 2 grenades were widely used in Vietnam by US soldiers. These were fragmentation grenades. This means **shrapnel** burst from the grenade when it exploded.

US and South Vietnamese troops also used grenades that released chemicals. The M15 white **phosphorus** smoke grenade was one. It exploded in a cloud of thick, white smoke. This smoke made it difficult for those nearby to breathe. Soldiers used these grenades to flush NLF soldiers out of hiding places in forests, tunnels, and caves.

Mines placed by both sides were often also hiding in forests and fields. They were buried or stuck into the

A US aircraft dropping a white phosphorus grenade

ground and connected to a trip wire. The bomb exploded when the wire was tripped. US troops often set up these mines around their campsites at night.

The NLF also often used mines. It dug holes in the ground and placed landmines inside. The holes were

The NLF often burned broken bamboo shoots to harden and sharpen them into punji sticks. Then, poison was sometimes smeared on the sharp end.

covered with dirt, grass, or straw. The weight of a **vehicle** or soldier stepping on the mine set off the explosive. The NLF placed mines along roads, in fields, and at the bottom of streams.

The NLF also used many other types of hidden traps to harm the enemy. These types of weapons are known as booby traps. Punji sticks were one type of booby trap.

Punji sticks were made by hammering long nails or sharpened sticks into a wooden block. These blocks were hidden on the ground. When a soldier stepped on one, the nails pierced his foot.

Sometimes punji sticks were set above doorways. They were connected to a wire. When a soldier tripped the wire, a spiked stick flew toward him.

US troops were armed with more advanced weaponry in Vietnam. But the NLF's low-tech defenses were very effective. Paired with the NLF's talent for hiding, these homemade weapons often **crippled** US troops.

TECH FACT

The NLF created tunnel systems in Vietnam. It used these tunnels to hide and execute surprise attacks.

CHEMICAL WARFARE

Vietnam's fields and forests were difficult to traverse due to mines and booby traps. But the **terrain** itself also created challenging conditions. Soldiers often had trouble spotting the enemy through Vietnam's thick forests. Chemical weapons were employed as a solution.

US troops used many types of chemical weapons in Vietnam. Several destroyed the leafy plants the enemy so often hid behind. These chemicals also killed the crops needed to feed NVA and NLF troops.

Agent Orange was one such chemical. It was sprayed from planes to kill plants. However, Agent Orange also got into the soil and water. For years after the war, this chemical has caused health problems in people. These include **cancer** and birth **defects**.

Napalm was another chemical US troops used in Vietnam. This liquid was mixed with gasoline to form a sticky gel. US pilots dropped napalm bombs from planes.

A US soldier blasts fiery napalm from a tank flamethrower.

The bombs exploded in flames, burning everything they touched. Napalm was also used in **flamethrowers**. Upon contact, napalm stuck to the skin. It caused painful burns. Napalm also poisoned the air and caused **asphyxiation**. It was responsible for killing many people, including nonmilitary Vietnamese citizens.

AIRCRAFT

US troops dropped more than 350,000 tons **(317,500 tonnes) of napalm bombs during the Vietnam War.** These bombs were dropped from several types of aircraft. One was the B-52 bomber.

This B-52's first military use was in Vietnam. It was used to support **infantry** by dropping bombs. This heavy bomber could carry up to 84 500-pound (227 kg) bombs in its bay. It could carry another 24 bombs on its wings.

One of the most advanced aircraft of the Vietnam War was the F-105 Thunderchief. It was equipped with a powerful radar system and flew very fast. The F-105 could reach a top speed of nearly 1,400 miles per hour (2,250 kmh). Like the B-52, the F-105 could hold several tons of bombs in its bay and on its wings.

Perhaps the most important aircraft in the war were helicopters. These aircraft had been influential during the

Thunderchiefs drop bombs on an enemy military base over North Vietnam on June 14, 1966.

Korean War. But they were at the heart of the action in Vietnam.

Unlike planes, helicopters can fly sideways and directly up and down. And they don't need a long runaway to take off or land. In Vietnam, this meant they could get in and out of thick forests more easily.

These features made helicopters useful for dropping troops and supplies into combat zones. These aircraft

could quickly transport injured
soldiers to safety. Helicopters also
sometimes fought directly above
ground troops during battle.

One of the most common helicopters of the time was
the Bell UH-1 or "Huey." It could fly at lower altitudes and
speeds than other aircraft. The Huey was heavily armed
to support troops with its strong firepower.

Later in the war, the NVA and NLF developed a
powerful anti-aircraft system. They used these weapons

THE BATTLE OF AP BAC

On January 2, 1963, the South Vietnamese and US armies attacked NLF members in the village of Ap Bac, South Vietnam. US helicopters were used to great advantage in this battle. The aircraft dropped about 2,500 South Vietnamese soldiers directly into the village. This took the 300 NLF soldiers by great surprise.

Helicopters gave the South Vietnamese an edge. The South Vietnamese troops also outnumbered the NLF. But the South Vietnamese were poorly trained and lost the battle.

In the end, 18 NLF members were killed in the battle. The smaller NLF army killed 80 South Vietnamese soldiers. It injured more than 100 others. Three US advisors were also killed. The NLF also shot down five US helicopters. US troops had to send more helicopters to rescue the surviving soldiers from the village.

to battle US aircraft. Some of the deadliest weapons they used were surface-to-air **missiles**.

The SA-2 guideline was one type of missile. It was 35 feet (11 m) long. The missile could soar more than 90,000 feet (27,400 m) at four times the speed of sound. Its blast destroyed everything within 300 yards (274 m). During the Vietnam War, this included countless US aircraft.

(7)

DEFEAT

By the late 1960s, it became clear the war was far from over. Then, a surprise attack in 1968 was a turning point. Called the Tet Offensive, it involved the attack of more than 100 South Vietnamese towns by the NVA and NLF.

Americans watched video of these attacks on their televisions. They were shocked by what they saw. US President Lyndon B. Johnson began to limit US bombings in Vietnam. He also called for peace talks. But when Richard Nixon took office in 1969, he increased bombings overseas. Americans grew more upset.

Finally, the Paris Peace Accords were signed in 1973. They called for the withdrawal of US forces from Vietnam. Two years later, Saigon fell to the NVA. North and South Vietnam were reunited as a communist nation. However, even today, deep feelings of division remain.

The war caused great damage in Vietnam. Millions of its people died and much of the land was destroyed. It took years to rebuild the economy.

A captured US army officer is released by an NVA officer in 1973.

Despite the many losses, the Vietnam War resulted in some **technological** gains. The M60 became a standard weapon of war in future conflicts. Helicopters affected the Vietnam War in a major way. Since then, these aircraft have become important tools of war. The technologies used in the Vietnam War have since helped save many lives and secure battle victories.

GLOSSARY

accuracy — the state or quality of being free from error.

aluminum — a silver-colored, lightweight metal. It is used in making machinery and other products.

ammunition — bullets, shells, cartridges, or other items used in firearms and artillery.

asphyxiation — a condition of not being able to breathe due to a lack of oxygen, causing death.

automatic — moving or acting by itself.

cancer — any of a group of often deadly diseases marked by harmful changes in the normal growth of cells. Cancer can spread and destroy healthy tissues and organs.

cease-fire — a temporary stopping of hostile activities.

conventional — traditional or used by most people.

cripple — to cause something or someone to work less efficiently.

defect — a physical problem.

flamethrower — a weapon that shoots streams of burning liquid.

fleet — a group of ship or airplanes under one command.

guerilla — when a small force uses creative means to try and influence or affect a larger force.

infantry — soldiers trained and organized to fight on foot.

Korean War — a war fought in North and South Korea from 1950 to 1953. The US government sent troops to help South Korea.

missile — a weapon that is thrown or projected to hit a target.

negotiation (nih-GOH-shee-ay-shun) — a discussion to work out an agreement about the terms of something.

paddy — wet land in which rice is grown.

personnel — the people employed by a certain organization.

phosphorus — a poisonous chemical that burns when it is touched by air.

reconnaissance — military observation of the enemy.

shrapnel — small metal pieces that scatter from a bomb.

skirmish — a brief and usually unplanned fight during a war.

tactic — a method of moving military forces in battle.

technology (tehk-NAH-luh-jee) — machinery and equipment developed for practical purposes using scientific principles and engineering. Something that relates to or uses technology is technological.

terrain — a particular type of land.

vehicle — something used to carry or transport. Cars, trucks, airplanes, and boats are vehicles.

warfare — methods and weapons used to fight a war.

WEBSITES

To learn more about **Military Technologies**, visit **booklinks.abdopublishing.com**. These links are routinely monitored and updated to provide the most current information available.

INDEX